READ ON

M000100822

I Like It Here

by Lada Josefa Kratky

NATIONAL
GEOGRAPHIC

School Publishing

I am Kim. See my kids, Kit and Kip.

They like it here a lot.

cod

They get good cod.
They have a good bed.

I am Kam. See my kids, Kat and Kev.

They like it here a lot.

The cubs get fed. Kat and Kam take a nap.

They like it here a lot.